Series 117

This is a Ladybird Expert book, one of a series of titles for an adult readership. Written by some of the leading lights and outstanding communicators in their fields and published by one of the most trusted and well-loved names in books, the Ladybird Expert series provides clear, accessible and authoritative introductions, informed by expert opinion, to key subjects drawn from science, history and culture.

The Publisher would like to thank the following for the illustrative references for this book:
Pages 17 & 27 (soldiers in foreground): *Images of War, The Invasion of Sicily 1943.* Page 35: US Army photo – public domain. Page 37: © National Library of New Zealand. Page 41: Body shot of Leese © The Royal Aeronautical Society (National Aerospace Library) / Mary Evans Picture Library; Reese's head – IWM TR 1759; © British Pathé Ltd, Film ID 1386.12.

Every effort has been made to ensure images are correctly attributed; however, if any omission or error has been made please notify the Publisher for correction in future editions.

MICHAEL JOSEPH

UK | USA | Canada | Ireland | Australia
India | New Zealand | South Africa

Michael Joseph is part of the Penguin Random House group of companies
whose addresses can be found at global.penguinrandomhouse.com

Penguin
Random House
UK

First published 2021

001

Text copyright © James Holland, 2021

All images copyright © Ladybird Books Ltd, 2021

The moral right of the author has been asserted

Printed in Italy by L.E.G.O. S.p.A.

The authorized representative in the EEA is Penguin Random House Ireland,
Morrison Chambers, 32 Nassau Street, Dublin D02 YH68

A CIP catalogue record for this book is available from the British Library

ISBN: 978–0–718–18654–8

www.greenpenguin.co.uk

The War in Italy

James Holland

**with illustrations by
Keith Burns**

Ladybird Books Ltd, London

At dusk on 9 July 1943, the Allied invasion force was approaching Sicily. Those on board the fleet could see Mount Etna rising into the sky in the distance. Operation HUSKY was the largest amphibious invasion ever mounted: some 160,000 British, American and Canadian troops and more than 14,000 vehicles in over 2,590 vessels of varying sizes and supported by a staggering 3,600 aircraft. This mammoth undertaking had set sail from Alexandria in Egypt, from northern Tunisia and tiny Malta, brutally besieged in the first years of the war but now the launch pad for the Allied invasion of Axis-dominated Europe.

Above the invasion fleet was an impressive armada of gliders and aircraft carrying paratroopers. It was the first time the Allies had mounted a large-scale airborne operation, although this part of the invasion was soon to turn into a fiasco. The Allied airborne troops were all highly trained and motivated, but were being delivered by woefully ill-prepared aircrew who had been given little chance to train with the troops they were due to deliver, and especially not at night. To make matters worse, strong winds had started to whip up over the Mediterranean.

American paratroopers from the 82nd Airborne Division were to capture key features that would then make the tasks of the landing US infantry that followed easier, while British glider troops were to secure intact a key bridge, Ponte Grande, to the south of the city of Syracuse. In the event, both paratroopers and glider troops were tragically scattered to the four winds. Only 425 out of 3,500 paratroopers even got close to their objectives, while only four out of 144 gliders landed on their drop zone. It was a shambles and a poor start to the invasion.

The Allied invasion force approaching Sicily at dusk on 9 July 1943.

It had been agreed at the Casablanca Conference back in January 1943 that, after winning the war in North Africa, the Allies would invade Sicily. The aim was to get a foothold in Europe, knock Italy out of the war and threaten Nazi Germany from southern Europe. The trouble was, victory in Tunisia was not completed until 13 May 1943 and planning for HUSKY, as the invasion was code-named, had to begin long before that and without any real knowledge of what the strength of enemy defence might be.

It was a mind-bogglingly complex operation that involved coalition air, land and naval forces. General Sir Harold Alexander, the Allied land commander, wanted to concentrate his forces as much as possible. On the other hand, Air Chief Marshal Sir Arthur Tedder, commander of Allied air forces, knew that having control of the skies was essential and that Sicily was awash with airfields in the east, west, centre and south. He hoped for multiple landings and for the ground troops to capture all the island's airfields swiftly.

There was also the need to keep the enemy guessing as to where they might strike. Complex deception plans were put in place to suggest the Allies would be landing in Sardinia or Greece but not Sicily. In the end, the plan for HUSKY went through eight evolutions, but it was finally agreed that British Eighth Army, under General Bernard Montgomery, should land in the south-east and the American Seventh Army, commanded by General George S. Patton, in the central-southern part of the island. Allied air forces would roam far and wide, destroying as many Axis aircraft as possible on the ground and in the air prior to the invasion.

The invasion of Sicily
10–23 July 1943

SCALE

0   80 km

50 miles

→ Allied advances

⊓⊔⊓⊔⊓ German detences

Palermo

Messina

SAN STEFANO LINE

Mt Etna

Catania

S I C I L Y

Catania Plain

Ponte Primisole

Licata

Gela

Syracuse

Allied air forces did superbly well. The tiny island of Pantelleria to the south-west of Sicily was bombed into submission by 11 June, while Sicilian airfields and communication centres were hammered so hard in the days leading up to the invasion that only just over 100 Axis fighters remained on the island by the time the invasion got under way. Other targets were hit across the Mediterranean.

The Italian dictator, Benito Mussolini, and Field Marshal Albert Kesselring, the German commander-in-chief in the Mediterranean, were both convinced the Allies would land in Sicily despite their deception measures and even though Hitler believed it would be in southern Greece. There were, however, sufficient doubts and differences of opinion in Axis minds that preparation was needed for every eventuality. By the end of the first week of July, Kesselring had two German divisions in Sicily, although the Hermann Göring Division had only just arrived. He placed it in the centre of the island and moved the 15th Panzer-Grenadier Division, which had been based centrally, to the west instead. This move was completed by 6 July but meant neither division knew the terrain in which it now found itself. This was to prove a critical mistake.

Overall command on the ground was left to the Italian General Alfredo Guzzoni, who had a number of infantry divisions as well as large numbers of coastal naval forces. What neither the Germans nor the Allies knew, however, was how well these more than 200,000 Italian troops would fight. Although the Italians were generally poorly trained, there were bunkers, large numbers of coastal gun batteries and other artillery and they would be fighting for Italian soil.

On paper, at any rate, Sicily looked a very tough nut for the Allies to crack, despite the success of the air forces.

Aerial battle over Sicily. Allied fighters shoot down Me109s and Macchi 202s.

Although the Americans faced fierce fighting at Gela, especially, broadly speaking the invasion went far better than the Allies could have hoped, and that was despite the chaos of the airborne assault. Although fewer than seventy British glider troops attacked Ponte Grande rather than 2,000, they not only secured the bridge but managed to hold on to it too. The Special Raiding Squadron – the SAS as they had been in North Africa – arriving by landing craft and led by Major Paddy Mayne, successfully scaled cliffs and destroyed three vital coastal batteries for the loss of just one dead and two wounded. It was a brilliantly carried out attack.

Meanwhile, British troops came ashore to very limited and sporadic opposition and swiftly moved inland. By nightfall, they were entering Syracuse, one of the key invasion objectives.

The next day, the Italian Livorno Division and the men of the Hermann Göring, some in massive Tiger tanks, counter-attacked at Gela and several German panzers almost reached the sea. Personally commanding the defence on the beach was General Patton and, thanks to his leadership, determined fighting from the Americans and the brilliant work of a group of anti-tank gunners, the Axis counter-attack was successfully repulsed.

By 12 July, General Dwight D. Eisenhower, the Supreme Allied Commander, was aboard a ship off the southern coast and, seeing thousands of vehicles and men already ashore, realized the Allies would now win on Sicily. Curiously, watching the same thing from a piece of high ground inland, was the German General Fridolin von Senger und Etterlin. He drew exactly the same conclusion as Eisenhower.

It would not be plain sailing for the Allies, however.

SRS attacking Capo Murro di Porco.

Montgomery's plan had been for Eighth Army to sweep up to Catania, a sizeable port on the east coast, then swiftly on to Messina in the north-eastern part of the island, where Sicily lay only a mile or so from the boot of mainland Italy. Patton's Seventh Army was to support Eighth Army's flanks. The key was to get on to the plain of Catania – one of the few flat parts of the island – quickly, before the enemy regained their balance.

First, though, it was essential to ensure the invasion did not fail. That trumped all other considerations. This was why Alexander had supported the decision to front-load the invasion with troops rather than vehicles. As it turned out, Italian resistance was less than had been feared and so the British infantry were left to move up towards Catania largely on foot. Sicily in July was scorching hot, diseases such as dysentery and malaria were rife, water was in short supply and the Germans very swiftly reorganized themselves.

German troops, under Colonel Wilhelm Schmalz – one of the highly experienced and capable combat commanders who made German troops such a tough proposition – formed blocking forces along the main axes of the British advance. Delaying the British allowed Kesselring, largely cutting General Guzzoni out of the loop, to move the bulk of his forces back to a rough defensive line overlooking the Catania Plain and with their guns set up in the foothills of Mount Etna.

At the same time, leading units of the 1st Fallschirmjäger – Parachute – Division were flown in to secure Ponte Primosole, the one key bridge on the Catania Plain that led north. Ironically, British paratroopers were also dropped to seize the very same bridge. British and German airborne troops landed on the same drop zones just hours apart.

German Fallschirmjäger landing on drop zones near the Primosole Bridge.

A bitter and bloody battle followed around Primosole Bridge. In the extreme heat, the dead soon began to putrefy. Lieutenant David Fenner, whose 6th Durham Light Infantry were thrown into the battle on the night of 15 July, was shocked by the scenes of carnage and sight of flies feasting on twisted carcasses.

The British finally took the bridge on 17 July, but precious time had been lost. Not only was the bridge repeatedly put out of action in the days that followed, but the Germans had regained their balance and were now firmly dug in overlooking the Catania Plain. Repeated attempts to break through were stopped in their tracks.

This prompted a rethink by Montgomery, who now pushed forward the Canadians and the 51st Highland Division to try to break through further west of the plain. Here, though, the terrain was much hillier and greatly favoured the defender. The Canadian Hastings and Prince Edward's Regiment – known as the 'Hasty Ps' – were given the task of attacking one such hilltop strongpoint, the town of Assoro. Led by Major Lord Tweedsmuir, son of the adventure writer John Buchan, they scaled an almost vertical side of the mountain by night, took the observation post on the summit and then held out until Allied artillery finally forced the Germans to pull back. It was an extraordinary action, but Assoro was followed by another hilltop to be captured, then another and another.

Monty's left hook had forced the Americans into a supporting role, which did not please General Patton. On 17 July he visited Alexander and asked to be allowed to head westwards to capture Palermo.

Canadians assaulting Assoro.

14

Patton was given his wish, and with most German troops now behind a defensive position, the San Stefano Line, which cut off the entire north-east of Sicily, the Americans swiftly overwhelmed the remaining Italian forces in the west of the island. Palermo was taken in triumph on 22 July. Helping the Americans had been the tactical support given by the Mafia, brought to heel under Mussolini but now given a new lease of life by the Allies. Don Calò Vizzini, the senior Mafia figure on Sicily, encouraged Sicilian troops to lay down their arms. Most did.

The main battle, however, continued along the San Stefano Line. In the sweltering heat and dust the fighting was brutal. Thin soil and rocky ground meant stone splinters from mortars and artillery were lethal for both sides. On the Catania Plain, meanwhile, the British were losing more casualties to malaria than to battle. The Allies might have had superiority in numbers, fire-power and air support, but the landscape favoured the defenders. Sicily was a tough, demoralizing place in which to fight.

Hitler had now ordered one of his best commanders, General Valentin Hube, to take command of XIV Panzer Corps on Sicily with two more divisions. His brief was to hold Sicily for as long as possible. Known by his men as 'Der Mann', Hube now swiftly bypassed Guzzoni, absorbed Italian artillery units into his own, and prepared further defensive lines in the north-east of the island.

For the Italians, meanwhile, Sicily was proving the straw that broke the camel's back. They wanted out of a war for which most had never had much enthusiasm and from an alliance with partners they mostly despised.

American troops enter Palermo.

On 24 July, the Fascist Grand Council voted to overthrow Mussolini. Initially refusing to resign, he was forced to stand down the following day by the Italian king, Victor Emmanuel. Although the new government, under Marshal Pietro Badoglio, told their ally they would continue to fight alongside them, these were empty words, as the Germans were well aware. Almost immediately, the Italians began armistice negotiations with the Allies, while at the same time the Germans prepared Operation AXIS, the occupation of Italy and Greece, for the moment the Italians pulled out of the war.

While these high-level events were going on, the battle continued to rage on Sicily. Agira, Regalbuto, Troina and Centuripe became bywords for the bloody, bitter and attritional fighting as the British, Canadians and Americans wrested one hilltop town after another. Catania was finally captured on 5 August.

The German defence was being ground down, however. Fortunately for them, the north-east of Sicily narrowed to a tip, which meant that, as they fell back to the next defensive line, fewer men were needed to defend it. Remaining Italian troops began evacuating across the narrow Strait of Messina in the first week of August, and the Germans on the 11th. With some 333 anti-aircraft guns massed on each side of the Strait, it was impossible for Allied bombers to fly in and attack at low-level or for naval warships to get close.

In all, 62,000 Italians and 39,569 German troops were safely evacuated, along with 9,605 vehicles. Although the Allies were disappointed that so many enemy troops escaped, thirty-six days in which to capture a heavily defended island such as Sicily had been a considerable victory.

German anti-aircraft gunners furiously defend the Strait of Messina.

That same day of victory, 17 August, Italian surrender negotiations were agreed. Although willing to switch sides, they were to be 'co-belligerents' rather than formal allies. That same day, the Allied Joint Chiefs of Staff also agreed to invade southern Italy.

The Americans had been reluctant to do this, as they were worried it was a further distraction from the main strategy, which was a cross-Channel invasion of Nazi-occupied France from southern England. However, General George Marshall, the US Chief of Staff and most senior general, came round to the idea for three main reasons. First, decrypts of German coded traffic revealed that, if the Allies invaded, Hitler planned to pull his forces back to a line some 200 miles north of Rome between Pisa and Rimini. This suggested the Allies could easily capture the Italian capital, a major psychological victory.

The second was the chance to capture a group of airfields in central-southern Italy at Foggia. Heavy strategic bombers could then be based there, allowing the noose to be further tightened around Nazi Germany. In particular, Germany's one oilfield, at Ploesti in Romania, could be bombed from Foggia. Finally, it was also hoped fighting in Italy would draw German troops away from north-west Europe before the invasion of France, planned for the following May.

Without telling the Italians the exact details or timings of their plans, the Allies intended to land Montgomery's Eighth Army in southern Italy first, followed by an armistice announcement a few days later and then, the following day, Lieutenant-General Mark Clark's US Fifth Army would make an amphibious invasion of Italy at Salerno, just to the south of Naples. It was confidently expected that General Alexander's 15th Army Group would be in Rome by Christmas.

The Italians sign the armistice.

The invasion of Italy was still fraught with risk, however. There were some seventeen German divisions in Italy by this time – in Sicily there had never been more than four. The Germans knew Italy was likely to quit the war, which was why they had prepared Operation AXIS to flood both Italy and Greece with German troops and disarm the Italian armed forces the moment they did so. And actually, the strategy was initially to resist an Allied invasion but then carry out a methodical withdrawal to the Pisa–Rimini Line. This was based on the assumption that the Allies would never try to fight their way up the peninsula but instead would move north in a series of outflanking manoeuvres by sea. In reality, the Allies had nothing like the shipping and landing craft the Germans thought they had – much of that used for Sicily had already been sent to the Pacific or back to Britain. The cross-Channel invasion planned for May 1944 remained the strategic priority for the Allies.

Eighth Army landed on the toe of Italy to almost no opposition on 3 September, while British paratroopers captured the port of Taranto, complete with much of the Italian fleet. The armistice was announced on 8 September, much to the surprise of the Italians, who for some reason had become convinced it would be on 12 September. Caught completely off guard, the king and Marshal Badoglio fled Rome, while German troops swept in and successfully disarmed much of the Italian Army. They would now be no help to the Allies.

The landings at Salerno took place the following day, but because of the shortage of shipping, Mark Clark's Fifth Army came ashore with just three divisions in the first assault, of which two were British. It was very nearly a catastrophic failure.

British paratroopers at Taranto.

Meanwhile, German commando troops had sprung Mussolini from his prison in the Gran Sasso in the southern Apennines and installed him as a puppet dictator of the new fascist Socialist Republic of Italy – the RSI. It meant the north was subject to even stricter Nazi-dominated control.

To the south, the Allies landed successfully at Salerno, but their situation quickly became precarious. Eighth Army was advancing from the toe, but was still some way to the south, while the lack of any support from the Italians meant Field Marshal Kesselring decided to throw the weight of the newly formed German Tenth Army against Salerno.

Although the beaches were good for landing, they lay in a semi-circular amphitheatre surrounded by hills from which every move could be seen. British and American troops also landed too far apart to mutually support one another, and by 11 September the Germans were furiously counter-attacking with five divisions. At one point, the situation became so critical that General Clark came ashore and personally took command of some anti-tank guns. Eighth Army was urged to hurry from the south and massive extra air and naval support was brought in. Allied fire-power from the air and sea made all the difference. By 16 September, General Heinrich von Vietinghoff, the German Tenth Army commander, decided it was time to pull back. One last counter-attack was made on 17 September to mask their withdrawal, but the Battle of Salerno was over. It was not, though, the start to the Italian campaign that the Allies had hoped for. Nor was it about to get any easier for them.

Hitler, stirred by the determined defence at Salerno, now changed his orders and told Kesselring he wanted him to fight for every yard. There was no longer to be a swift retreat to the Pisa–Rimini Line.

The Salerno landings.

The trouble was, the Allies had set their strategy in stone: the overall priority was still to be the capture of Foggia and the build-up of the new Fifteenth Air Force. That meant giving them, rather than Alexander's armies, the lion's share of shipping capacity and fuel. To make matters worse for the Allies, the Mediterranean sunshine in which the Italian campaign had been planned rapidly disappeared, replaced instead by weeks of endless rain and, with it, mud. Although the Foggia airfields were in their hands by 1 October, the narrow, mountainous nature of Italy meant it was not an easy place in which to advance. From the mountains, rivers ran down to the sea, across the path of the Allies.

Highly mechanized and using a large number of vehicles, the Allies needed roads. There were, however, only four main routes leading to Rome. One passed through the centre, which was too mountainous. Another ran along the eastern Adriatic coast and a third beside the western Ionian coast; the latter was narrow and the mountains too close for manoeuvre. Only one other main road was available: Highway 1, the old Roman Via Casilina, which ran north–south from Rome inland from the west coast. All were fairly easy for the Germans to block.

In the rain and mud, Eighth Army began pushing up the Adriatic Coast, while Fifth Army headed up the Via Casilina. All the way, bridges were blown and the roads lined with mines and booby traps. The confidence and hopes with which Italy had been invaded were quickly dampening. By Christmas, Fifth Army was still some 70 miles south of Rome. The River Volturno had been crossed but now they faced a major new defensive position: the Gustav Line.

A column of troops moving over a Bailey bridge through the rain, mud and mountains.

While the Allies had been slogging their way northwards, the Germans had been creating a formidable defensive position that ran the width of Italy. A network of bunkers, mines, wire, mortar pits and gun positions, it was strongest around the town of Cassino. Here the Via Casilina emerged through narrow passes into the Liri Valley, an expanse around 5 miles wide that ran much of the way to Rome. Highway 1 hugged its eastern side, passing through Cassino. Towering above was the Monte Cassino massif, the end of the mountain spur on which stood a famous Benedictine monastery.

As the Allies were all too aware, the Germans had observers and guns aimed on any attempt by Fifth Army to break through into the Liri Valley. General Clark first tried to burst through by forcing a crossing over the River Rapido at the southern end of the valley. The 36th Texas Division was given this dubious honour and were cut to pieces in the process. After the disaster of the 'Bloody Rapido', an outflanking manoeuvre was attempted further up the coast at Anzio on 21 January 1944. This involved collecting precious shipping needed for the planned Normandy invasion, but although a bridgehead was secured, the attacking force was not strong enough to force the Germans to abandon the Gustav Line.

Next, at the end of January, Clark sent the 34th 'Red Bull' Division up on to the Monte Cassino massif, while the French Expeditionary Corps, largely made up of colonial North African troops, attacked further east in the mountains around Monte Abate. In the rain, cold and brutal conditions, the fighting was bitter and costly. Both the French and the Red Bulls made important gains but were unable to dislodge the Germans from the heights.

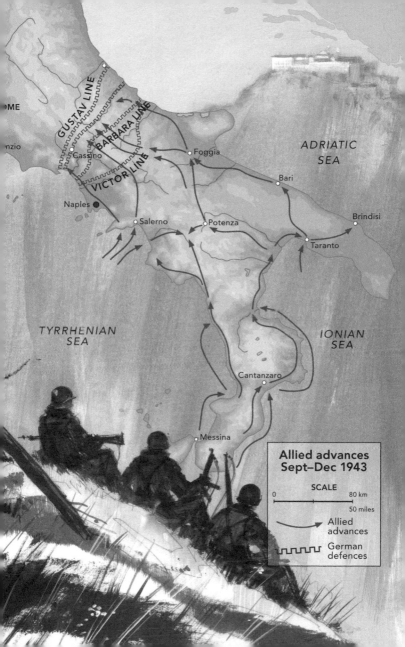

ME

nzio

GUSTAV LINE

BARBARA LINE

VICTOR LINE

Cassino

Naples

Salerno

Potenza

Foggia

Bari

Brindisi

Taranto

ADRIATIC SEA

TYRRHENIAN SEA

Cantanzaro

Messina

IONIAN SEA

Allied advances Sept–Dec 1943

SCALE

0   80 km

50 miles

⟶ Allied advances

⌐⌐⌐⌐ German defences

The Anzio landings had been meant to relieve the pressure at Cassino, but in February a further attack was made on the massif in an effort to take the strain off the beleaguered troops in the bridgehead. By this time, the Gustav Line at Monte Cassino had been reinforced with paratroopers of the 1st Fallschirmjäger Division, and Major-General Francis Tuker, the 4th Indian Division commander, suggested instead attacking further east where the enemy was less strong, cutting the massif and then isolating it. His immediate superior, Lieutenant-General Bernard Freyberg, commander of the New Zealand Corps, was unfamiliar with mountain warfare and so disregarded Tuker's idea. Instead, he ordered a direct attack on Monte Cassino – just as had been attempted before. This time, though, the strategic air forces, now based at Foggia, were called upon to plaster the position.

Tragically, the request to hit the entire massif did not reach the air forces and instead they focused on the beautiful monastery, which was pulverized. The Germans, who had not been using it, promptly created enviably strong positions amidst the rubble. Not only had an architectural and religious gem been destroyed, the enemy position on Monte Cassino had become stronger, not weaker. When the 4th Indian Division attacked, they predictably failed, just as previous attacks had done.

In March, Freyberg launched a further attack, this time hoping his troops would bludgeon their way through the town. The attack was also preceded by heavy bombing, which destroyed Cassino entirely. Once again, the rubble and ruins aided rather than hindered the Germans. A lot of men were being killed and wounded and an entire town smashed for very little gain. These were not the Allies' finest few weeks of battle.

The bombing of Monte Cassino.

Among the difficulties facing the Allies at Monte Cassino had been the weather as well as the terrain. Alexander's forces were highly mechanized and dependent on both fire and, increasingly, close air support provided by the tactical air forces. However, with the poor weather, air power had been less able to help. Nor had the troops on the ground been able to bring their huge advantage in mechanization to bear. Rather, pack mules had been the best means of transport.

But summer was on its way, and Alexander brought the bulk of Eighth Army, now commanded by General Oliver Leese, across the mountains alongside Fifth Army and began preparing a large-scale attack to smash the Gustav Line once and for all and capture Rome. Operation DIADEM was launched with a huge barrage of artillery fire on 11 May 1944.

The expectation was that Eighth Army would break through in the Liri Valley and speed down the Via Casilina. At the right moment, US V Corps at Anzio would then break out and, it was hoped, trap the bulk of the German Tenth Army in an encirclement.

The recently arrived II Polish Corps attacked on Monte Cassino. Theirs had been an extraordinary journey. Most had been captured by the Red Army back in September 1939 and sent to Gulags. After the German invasion of the USSR in June 1941, they had been released and told to muster in Kazakhstan, 2,000 miles to the south. There, many had suffered from an outbreak of typhus and malaria, but the survivors had made their way to Iraq, where the British had equipped and begun training them. After completing training in Palestine, they had been sent to Italy. Their first action was on Monte Cassino, which, after brutal fighting, they finally captured on 18 May.

The Poles fighting on Monte Cassino.

DIADEM did not develop as Alexander had imagined. Eighth Army struggled in the Liri Valley as they came up against the next line of defences, the so-called Senger Line, while the mass of streams and waterways all needed bridging, which took time. Lieutenant Ted Wyke-Smith was one engineer who helped build 26 Bailey bridges in 28 nights, an astonishing achievement; but despite this, the congestion of men and Eighth Army vehicles in the Liri Valley meant progress was slow.

Rather, it was the Free French, on their left and fighting through the mountains, and US II Corps, pushing along the west coast, who had the greatest success, pressing far ahead of the British and Canadians. It meant that by the time V Corps was ordered to burst out of the Anzio bridgehead, the remnants of the battered German Tenth Army were streaming down mountain roads further east. Not one German soldier retreated down the Via Casilina.

Instead of going all-out to cut Highway 1, as had been the original plan, General Clark now found his Fifth Army ahead of Eighth and facing a second German Army, the Fourteenth, dug in behind the next defensive position – the Caesar Line to the south of Rome. With this in mind, Clark now turned his forces to face them square on. To begin with, it seemed as though his men were banging against a brick wall, but then the Texans, recovered from their ordeal on the Rapido, found a gap in the German defences in the Alban Hills. Exploiting this weakness, the German line was swiftly blown wide open. Fourteenth Army fell back in disarray, and on 4 June Fifth Army entered Rome.

Fifth Army troops pass the Colosseum in Rome.

DIADEM was a huge victory – not only had German Tenth Army been badly mauled, but Fourteenth Army had been routed, making it a greater triumph than had originally been hoped. The cost to the Italians, however, was a terrible one. Cassino was entirely destroyed – barely a single building still stood – while the bomb craters were filled with stagnant water infested with malaria. Most of the surrounding villages and towns suffered similarly. The 60-mile stretch between Rome and Cassino was devastated. Many civilians had been killed and maimed and many more forced to flee to the mountains or find shelter in caves. 'To live in little caverns dug by us,' said Leonardo Bocale, 'without any facilities for hygiene, without a life, without knowing what our future could be, tossed like animals . . . we were abandoned: culturally, materially, spiritually.'

A stain on the Allied victory was the treatment of Italian civilians by men of the French Expeditionary Corps, who went on the rampage – raping, stealing and murdering untold numbers. These troops had fought superbly, yet in the flush of victory they ran amok. They were not the first troops in history to do so, nor would they be the last, but their actions added to the torment of the Italians, most of whom the previous September had thought the war was over. The fallacy of that belief had been brutally exposed.

Elsewhere in the south, now largely under Allied Military Government, inflation was out of control, food scarce and much of the infrastructure destroyed. Gangsters ran the black market. With many men either prisoners-of-war or transported to Germany as forced labour, it was left to the women to try to keep their families alive. They were paying a terrible price for Mussolini's entry into the war back in 1940.

Italian civilians suffered terribly in the fighting between Cassino and Rome.

Meanwhile, the Allied armies in Italy were slogging their way north from Rome and initially making great strides as the Germans fell back in disarray. In this narrow, mountainous country, however, it did not take long, nor many troops, for the shattered remnants of their two armies to set up blocking lines.

More German soldiers and supplies were hurriedly sent south through the Alps, while labourers continued to build the twin defensive lines of the Gothic Line, a truly formidable position that ran the width of the country and had always been seen as Germany's main line of defence in Italy.

First, though, came the Trasimeno Line in southern Tuscany and Umbria. A ten-day battle from 20 to 30 June saw the Allies bludgeon their way through at a mile a day before encountering numerous blocking lines as they headed to Florence. All the way, climbing blue in the distance, were the peaks of the Apennines, a constant reminder of what faced them to the north.

Florence, declared an 'open city' by Kesselring, was still contested by the Germans. All the bridges across the River Arno were blown except the beautiful Ponte Vecchio, too narrow, in any case, for military traffic. Italian partisans also tussled with fascist militia. Not until 4 August was the city finally captured by the Allies.

By this time, Alexander had lost a quarter of his forces to Operation DRAGOON, the Allied invasion of southern France. He had argued in vain that it was better to exploit the success of DIADEM and use the morale of victory and momentum to push through the Gothic Line that summer and then on through the Alps, either into France or the Balkans.

German Fallschirmjäger defending
the north bank of the River Arno in Florence.

The same day that Florence fell, Field Marshal Alexander met with General Oliver Leese, the British Eighth Army commander, at Orvieto airfield. It was a scorching hot day, so they talked under the wing of a Dakota aircraft, which offered some shade. The plan had been for Eighth and Fifth Army to continue fighting side by side to assault the Gothic Line in the centre.

Leese, though, now suggested moving Eighth Army to the Adriatic coast, where the mountains were less pronounced and where the Via Adriatica, the main coast road, could be the prime axis of advance. Alexander wanted his army commander to fight on ground of his choosing and was also aware of tensions between Leese and Clark, so agreed. But it meant a two-week delay in attacking while Eighth Army moved across Italy.

Leese had intended to use his V Corps along the coast – it was his strongest, with five divisions – with the Canadians in the hills on their left flank. However, it was pointed out to him that the Germans were now experts at blowing bridges and mining roads, so, at the last moment, he switched them around. The Canadians, however, had only two divisions and the Via Adriatica was still the main axis of advance for Eighth Army and, because it did not run through mountains, had been the main reason for switching the line of attack to the coast. Now, V Corps, with its strength, scale, heavy armour and vehicles, was to advance inland, across narrow winding dirt roads. It was not a good decision, because the Canadians did not have the strength in depth to push through along the Via Adriatica, whereas V Corps had.

Eighth Army began its assault of the Gothic Line on 25 August.

Alexander and Leese meet at Orvieto airfield.

Eighth Army managed to get through the first defences of the Gothic Line, Green I, by 2 September, but then, as Kesselring reinforced this part of the front, German resistance stiffened. Eighth Army reached Green II and was held up at the Coriano Ridge. V Corps was struggling in the foothills of the Apennines, and the Canadians were running out of steam. And it had begun to rain.

Meanwhile, Fifth Army had captured Pisa and pushed the Germans back to the Gothic Line in the centre and west. There were two main inland passes through the mountains: the Futa Pass was the easier route, but Clark decided to surprise the enemy by attacking through the narrower Giogo Pass. This was protected on either side by Monticelli to the west and Monte Altuzzo to the east. Although not held in any strength by the 4th Fallschirmjäger Division, it was none the less a daunting objective for the Americans of the 91st and 85th Divisions. Despite the attackers having formidable artillery and close air support, these peaks could be taken only by infantrymen slogging their way up narrow ridges and prising out each machine-gun nest and mortar position one by one.

Clark's men attacked on 12 September and, after a bloody and brutal battle in which both Germans and Americans fought heroically and with terrible casualties, the Giogo Pass was captured on 18 September. The bodies of many hundreds who fought there have never been recovered.

In the rain, the Allied armies continued to batter their way against the second line of German defences. During its assault on Monte Grande, the US 88th Division lost nearly 10,000 casualties in two weeks' fighting. Each peak fought for was an epic of grit, determination and sacrifice.

The Americans assaulting Monte Altuzzo.

Civil war had now effectively broken out in the north of Italy. Young men who did not want to be called up into SS police battalions or Mussolini's new divisions were increasingly fleeing to the mountains to become partisans. Although ill-trained, they rapidly became a major thorn in the side of the Germans, who, suffering from relentless Allied shelling and fighter-bomber attacks, now faced no let-up away from the front line either. Both German troops and fascist militias became embroiled in *rastrellamenti* – round-up operations to try to crush these insurgents. Kesselring reckoned partisans killed at least 30,000 German troops – over two divisions. He instigated a brutal rule of terror in which ten civilians were summarily executed for every one German killed. The beautiful towns of northern Italy were lined with hanged corpses, while mountain villages such as Sant'Anna di Stazzema and San Terenzo became scenes of appalling civilian massacres.

Many partisans were highly politicized, and often communist, but the Stella Rossa, operating in and around the Monte Sole massif to the south of Bologna, were a rare exception. Led by the charismatic 'Lupo', over the summer of 1944 they captured vital plans and made life very difficult for the Germans.

By the end of September 1944, and with the front just 10 miles to the south, the Stella Rossa had become an increasing problem. On the 29th, through the mist and rain, a large *rastrellamento* was launched, led by men of the 16th Waffen-SS Division. Partisans, the elderly, women and children were all rounded up and shot, and their homes destroyed. In all, 762 were murdered. It was the largest single civilian massacre in all of western Europe during the war.

A group of Stella Rossa partisans.

Despite the loss of so many troops back in July, by the end of October Alexander's Allied armies had come within a stone's throw of breaking through the Gothic Line defences completely and bursting out into the Po Valley. Yet it was not to be. With the onset of winter and another bout of appalling weather, it proved tantalizingly beyond them. Casualties were simply too high and, as the secondary theatre since the Allied invasion of Normandy two days after the fall of Rome, Italy had not been the priority for reinforcements. As it was, Alexander had a staggering twenty-four different nationalities fighting in his armies, even including an infantry division from Brazil.

On 29 October, he briefed his commanders about his winter plan, which was to place his forces on to the defensive. This also meant ordering the partisans temporarily to lay down their arms and wait until the following spring. For these resistance fighters, this was a catastrophic blow. They now faced a long, bitterly cold winter as outlaws, with diminishing supplies, hunted by Nazi police and fascist militias.

Meanwhile, Field Marshal Alexander also now had to deal with the Allied liberation of Greece and the Aegean, and on 23 November he was promoted to Supreme Allied Commander, Mediterranean. He had no hesitation in recommending that Mark Clark replace him as Army Group commander in Italy.

Heavy snow fell on northern Italy that winter of 1944–5, but as spring slowly dawned, so Clark began preparing his forces for what would be the final offensive in Italy.

Allied advances June–Nov 1944

SCALE

0 — 80 km

50 miles

⌒ Allied advances

ᒑᒑᒑᒑ German defences

Verona

Padua

Venice

Po River

Parma

Bologna

Ravenna

Rimini

ADRIATIC SEA

Pisa

Florence

GUSTAV LINE

Ancona

Siena

Arezzo

TRASIMENO LINE

Grosseto

Orvieto

Terni

Pescara

ROME

The winter was once again bitter. In the mountains, snow lay thick on the ground, making life miserable for all. Mussolini, still puppet dictator in the north, had become subdued and withdrawn, sensing the end was near, while General Karl Wolff, the senior SS commander in Italy, was even actively pursuing secret peace talks with the Allies. This was something Kesselring was not willing to countenance, however, which meant there would still be one last major battle.

By the beginning of March, Clark had crystallized his plans, once more favouring a two-fisted approach, with a big push by Fifth Army in the centre and with Eighth Army attacking at two places. One of these would involve crossing Lake Comacchio to the north of Ravenna, using 'fantail' amphibious tanks. The key, Clark realized, was to build up as much strength as possible while at the same time denying supplies to the enemy, then to hit them swiftly and very hard.

Since resources in northern Italy were, by this time, extremely scarce, most German supplies had to come from the Reich and south through the Alpine Brenner Pass. Allied air forces hammered this route, despite facing nearly 1,000 anti-aircraft guns in the narrow valley. Their efforts paid off. The previous autumn an average of thirty-eight trains had passed through each day, but by March 1945 the figure was just eight. Fuel supplies had dwindled to almost nothing.

At the same time, the Allies had been rearming the partisans and also sending increasing numbers of liaison officers, both American and British, to help train and coordinate their efforts. These irregulars were now instrumental in playing havoc with German supply lines.

By dawn on 9 April 1945, the Allies were ready. The final battle was about to begin.

American fighter-bombers shoot up German supplies heading south.

German resistance was initially stiff, with fierce battles all along the front, but the Allies kept bludgeoning their way through. Eighth Army successfully crossed Lake Comacchio, outflanking German positions, while on 20 April Bologna finally fell. Despite orders to the contrary, von Vietinghoff now gave the signal for his armies to fall back across the River Po.

At this moment, the glue that had kept the German forces defending Italy so doggedly for over a year and a half finally gave way. Cohesion crumbled as the Germans fled in disarray, ruthlessly pursued by Allied fighter aircraft. Terrible scenes were played out at the Po. Vehicles were destroyed, equipment abandoned and horses shot, while many of those unable to cross on the few ferries available drowned trying to swim.

General Wolff was urging Kesselring and von Vietinghoff to surrender, but neither would do so without the authority of Hitler. Meanwhile, on 25 April Mussolini fled north, only to be captured by partisans and executed along with his mistress, Clara Petacci. Their bodies were brought to Milan and, with three other leading fascists, hung upside down from butcher's hooks. Partisans now exacted their revenge on thousands of fascists as brutal blood-letting took hold.

The German surrender was finally agreed on 29 April, without Hitler's authority and with Wolff presenting it to von Vietinghoff as a *fait accompli.* It took effect at 2 p.m. on 2 May. The long, bitter war in Italy was part of the wider and ultimately effective Allied strategy of tightening a noose around Nazi Germany. For all its brutality, the conflict there saw not only the end of fascism but tied down large numbers of German troops, materiel and resources right to the very end. The enormity of that sacrifice and achievement should not be forgotten.

German troops fleeing in retreat across the River Po.

Further Reading

GENERAL HISTORIES

Peter Caddick-Adams *Monte Cassino: Ten Armies in Hell* (Arrow, 2013)

James Holland *Italy's Sorrow* (HarperCollins, 2009)

James Holland *Sicily '43: The First Assault on Fortress Europe* (Bantam Press, 2020)

W. G. F. Jackson *The Battle for Italy* (Harper, 1967)

MEMOIRS

Alex Bowlby *The Recollections of Rifleman Bowlby* (Phoenix, 1999)

Mark Clark *Calculated Risk* (Enigma Books, 2007)

Iris Origo *War in the Val'Dorica* (Pushkin Press, 2017)

Johannes Steinhoff *The Straits of Messina* (Corgi, 1973)